MADAGASCAR

Mary N. Oluonye

Lerner Publications Company • Minneapolis

Lerner Publications Company
A division of Lerner Publishing Group, Inc.
241 First Avenue North
Minneapolis, MN 55401 U.S.A.

Website address: www.lernerbooks.com

Library of Congress Cataloging-in-Publication Data

Oluonye, Mary N.
    Madagascar / by Mary N. Oluonye.
        p.   cm. — (Country explorers)
    Includes index.
    ISBN 978–1–58013–601–3 (lib. bdg. : alk. paper)
    1. Madagascar—Juvenile literature. I. Title.
DT469.M25049 2010
    969.1—dc22   2009020568

Manufactured in the United States of America
1 – VI – 12/15/09

Table of Contents

MALAWI

Welcome!

Let's explore Madagascar! This country is one of the biggest islands in the world. It lies off the coast of southeastern Africa.

The Mozambique Channel separates Madagascar from Africa's mainland. The Indian Ocean washes Madagascar's northern, eastern, and southern coasts. The Comoros islands lie to the northwest.

Madagascar has many miles of beautiful beaches.

AFRICA

MOZAMBIQUE

COMOROS

MOZAMBIQUE CHANNEL

MADAGASCAR

MAROMOKOTRO PEAK

BETSIBOKA RIVER

CLIFF OF ANGAVO

CLIFF OF BONGOLAVA

CENTRAL HIGHLANDS

HIGHLANDS

MANGOKY RIVER

CLIFF OF ANGAVO

● Toamasina

Antananarivo (Tana) ★

INDIAN OCEAN

Madagascar

MILES
0   100

0   100
KILOMETERS

	rain forest
	mountains
	highlands
	deserts
	plains
★	country's capital

The Land

Madagascar's western coast is a low plain. It is dotted with beaches and swamps. Parts of the southwest are very dry. Tropical rain forests blanket the eastern coastal plain. These forests get a lot of rain.

Mountains, hills, and valleys make up the Central Highlands. This region runs from north to south through the middle of Madagascar.

Masoala National Park includes some of the rain forest of the northeastern coastal plains.

6

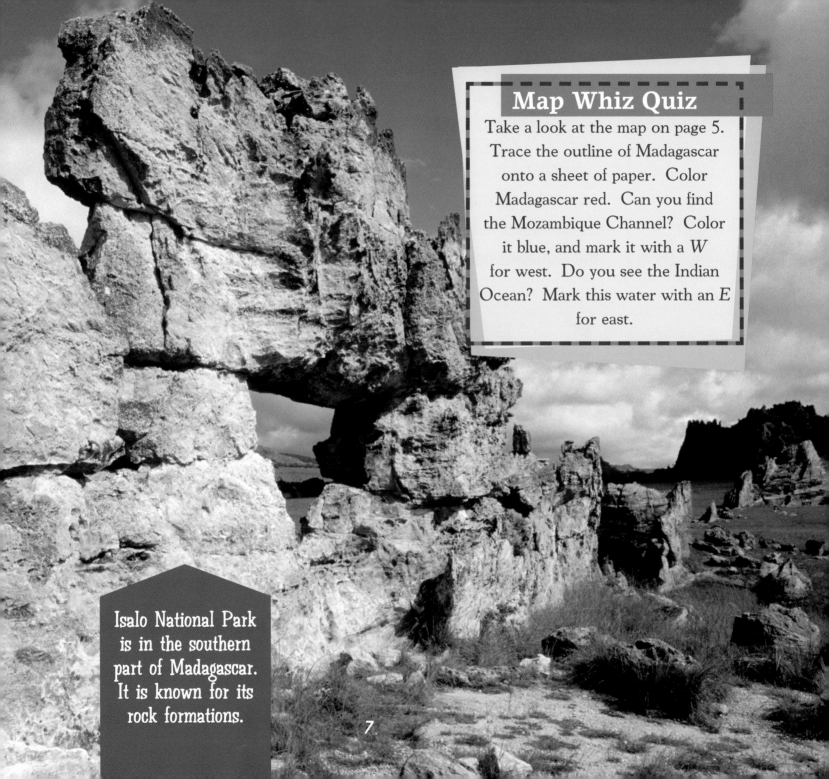

Map Whiz Quiz

Take a look at the map on page 5. Trace the outline of Madagascar onto a sheet of paper. Color Madagascar red. Can you find the Mozambique Channel? Color it blue, and mark it with a *W* for west. Do you see the Indian Ocean? Mark this water with an *E* for east.

Isalo National Park is in the southern part of Madagascar. It is known for its rock formations.

Two Seasons

Dress for fairly warm weather while you are in Madagascar. July and August are the coolest winter months. Even then, temperatures near the coasts are around 65°F (18°C). Parts of the highlands get colder.

The capital city of Antananarivo is in the highlands. These men are wearing long-sleeved shirts to stay warm.

Madagascar's eastern coast gets heavy rains between November and April.

Madagascar's summer lasts from November to April. It is the warmer, rainy season. Temperatures stay between 61°F and 84°F (16°C and 29°C). Summer winds called monsoons blow from the Indian Ocean. They bring big storms that dump rain on Madagascar's eastern coast.

Amazing Animals

Looking for strange animals? Do not miss the lemurs! They look like a mix between a monkey and a raccoon. You may have to search for them after dark. That is when some kinds of lemurs like to move around.

This ring-tailed lemur lives in the trees at Andringitra National Park in southeastern Madagascar.

The ocean around Madagascar is home to huge fish called coelacanths. Coelacanths have been around since the days of the dinosaurs!

Coelacanths were thought to be extinct (died out). Then some fishers found a live one in 1938.

Plants That Cure

Feel a cough coming on? Medicines can be made from some of Madagascar's plants. The periwinkle plant is in medicines that help people stop coughing. Periwinkle can also be used to treat bleeding problems, sore throats, and eye infections. Katrafay is another helpful plant. Add it to a hot bath to ease tired muscles.

This girl is holding a bouquet of periwinkles.

The ravenala is also known as the traveller's tree. Its leaf stems hold water that people can drink if they are really thirsty.

13

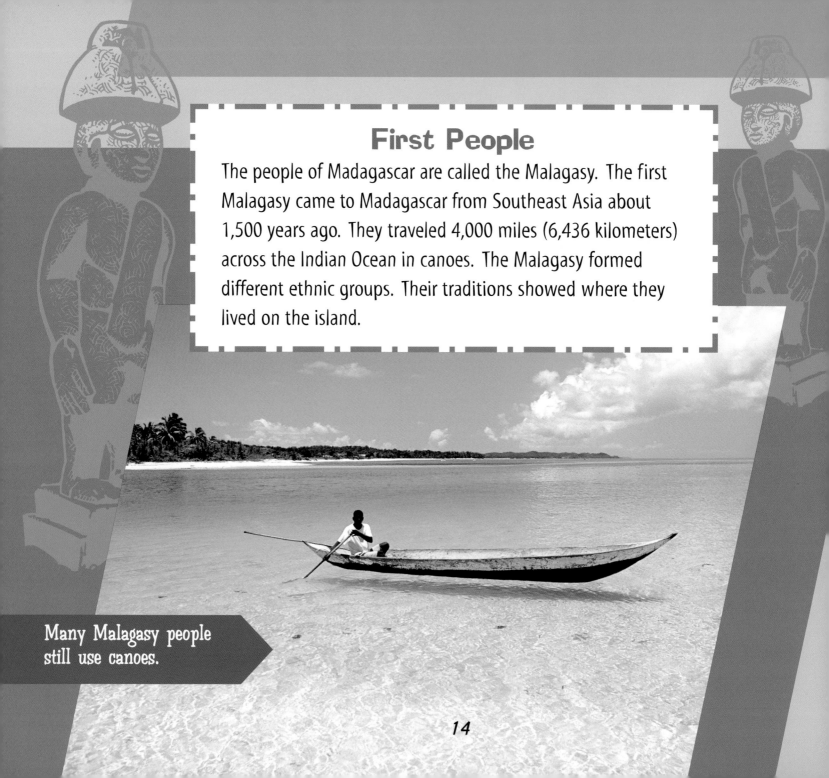

First People

The people of Madagascar are called the Malagasy. The first Malagasy came to Madagascar from Southeast Asia about 1,500 years ago. They traveled 4,000 miles (6,436 kilometers) across the Indian Ocean in canoes. The Malagasy formed different ethnic groups. Their traditions showed where they lived on the island.

Many Malagasy people still use canoes.

Some ethnic groups settled in the Central Highlands. People grow rice in large rice fields there.

15

We Are Malagasy

Madagascar is home to eighteen different ethnic groups! The Merina are the largest group. Many Merina work in the cities of the Central Highlands. They may own stores or other businesses. They may be lawyers or doctors.

Marc Ravalomanana was the first Merina elected president of Madagascar. He was president from 2002 to 2009.

16

The Betsimisaraka are fishers from the coasts. They are the second-largest group. The Betsileo grow crops in the Central Highlands.

These Betsimisaraka children live on the northeastern coast.

17

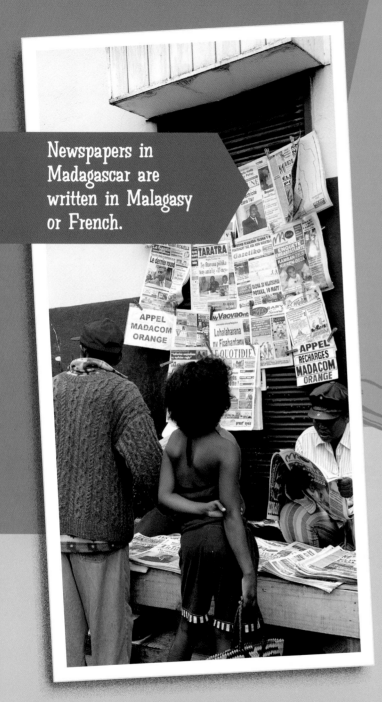

Newspapers in Madagascar are written in Malagasy or French.

Speak to Me

The language of the Malagasy people is also called Malagasy. It shares words with Indonesian and African languages. It has some Arabic, French, and English words too. The Malagasy alphabet looks like the English alphabet. But it does not have the letters *c, q, u, w,* or *x.*

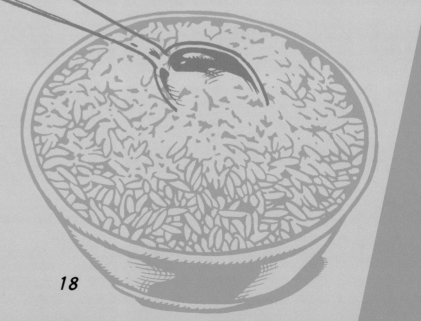

Talk to a Malagasy

Here are a few words and phrases in Malagasy.

English	Malagasy	Pronunciation
hello	Manao ahoana	MAH-noh OHN
good-bye	veloma	veh-LOOM
yes	eny	AY-nee
no	tsia	TSEE
please	azafady	ah-zah-FAHD

Many people also speak French. (This is because France ruled Madagascar from 1896 to 1960.) Malagasy and French are both official languages on the island. In 2007, Madagascar made English an official language too. But it is used mostly in government.

This Masoala National Park sign is written in French and Malagasy.

Lamba Time

What do you like to wear? Many Malagasy wear shorts and T-shirts. Some choose *lambas*. They wrap these long scarves around their bodies.

These people are wearing lambas or T-shirts. Malagasy men and women also love to wear hats.

This woman is weaving a lamba.

Malagasy women use a machine called a loom to weave lambas.
Weavers make lambas from silk, cotton, wool, or even grass.
Some lambas have patterns that show fruit, flowers, or shapes.

21

In the Country

About three-fourths of all Malagasy live in country villages. Kids live with parents, grandparents, great-grandparents, uncles, aunts, and cousins. Other family members usually live close by. Most country families grow their food in their own gardens and small fields.

This family lives in a village in southern Madagascar.

22

All in the Family

Here are the Malagasy words for family members.

grandfather	dadabe	(dah-dah-BAY)
grandmother	nenibe	(neh-nee-BAY)
father	dada	(DAH-dah)
mother	neny	(NEE-nee)
uncle	dadatoa	(dah-dah-TOO-ah)
aunt	nenitoa	(nee-nee-TOO-ah)
son	zanaka lahy	(ZAH-nah-kah LYE)
daughter	zanaka vavy	(ZAH-nah-kah VAH-vee)
brother	rahalahy	(rah-hah-LAH-hee)
sister	rahavavy	(rah-hah-VAH-vee)

Malagasy children help carry supplies for their family.

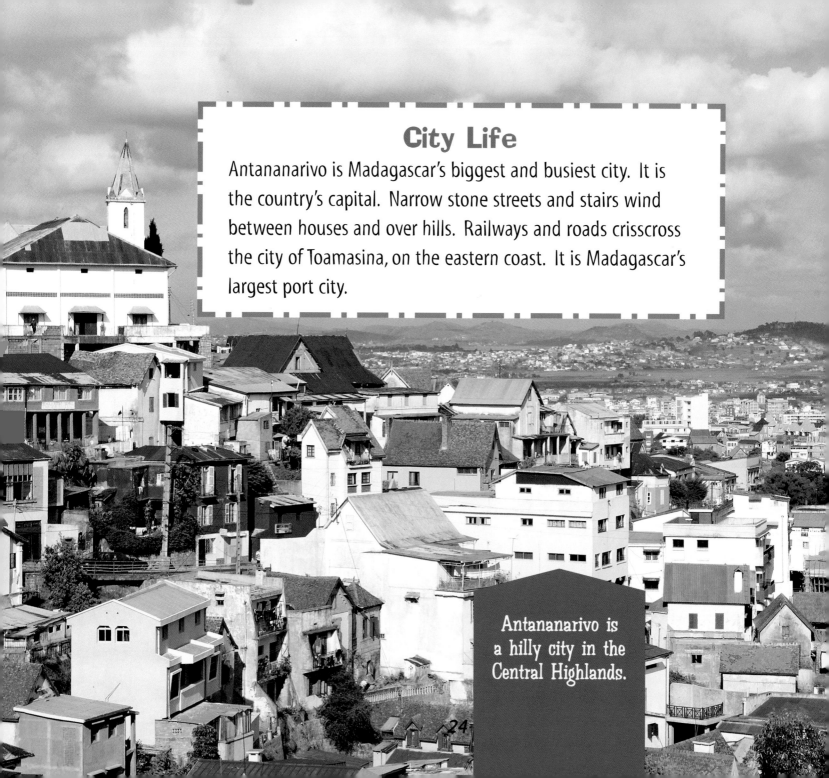

City Life

Antananarivo is Madagascar's biggest and busiest city. It is the country's capital. Narrow stone streets and stairs wind between houses and over hills. Railways and roads crisscross the city of Toamasina, on the eastern coast. It is Madagascar's largest port city.

Antananarivo is a hilly city in the Central Highlands.

24

Many people in Malagasy cities are poor. They work hard to make enough money to buy food. Some do not have jobs.

Many people in Toamasina work at the port, where boats arrive.

25

Marketplace

Visit an outdoor market to shop for food, clothes, or just about anything else you need. Tables and stands show woven rugs, mats, and hats. You may also find wood carvings, musical instruments, toys, and furniture for sale. Shoppers talk with sellers to get the best price.

Malagasy people buy and sell many things, such as colorful cloth, at an outdoor market.

These people are buying zebu cattle at a zebu market. Some zebu pull machinery. Others are raised for their meat.

27

On the Go

In a hurry? Then avoid cars in Madagascar. Poor roads make for a slow and bumpy ride. Lots of people just walk. Others may ride in a cart or wagon pulled by cows. In some cities, you can catch a ride in a *pousse-pousse*. It is a cart that a person pulls. (Its name means "push-push" in French.)

Pulling a pousse-pousse is hard work. That is why you will not find these carts in hilly cities such as Antananarivo.

For a longer trip into town or between cities, squeeze into a *taxi-brousse*. These minibuses or vans are usually crowded. Put your luggage on the roof, and climb in!

29

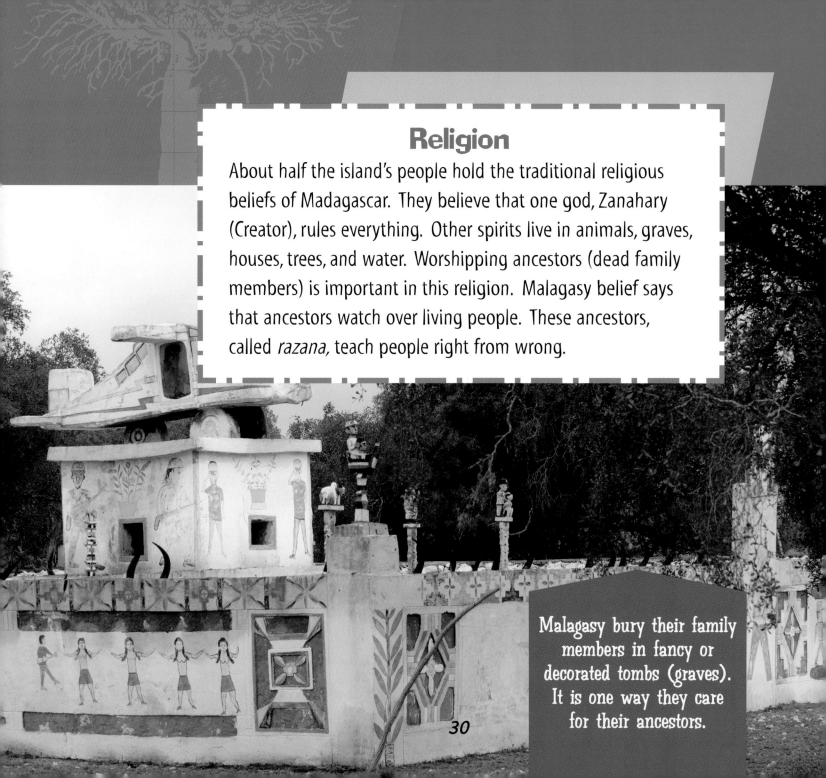

Religion

About half the island's people hold the traditional religious beliefs of Madagascar. They believe that one god, Zanahary (Creator), rules everything. Other spirits live in animals, graves, houses, trees, and water. Worshipping ancestors (dead family members) is important in this religion. Malagasy belief says that ancestors watch over living people. These ancestors, called *razana,* teach people right from wrong.

30

Malagasy bury their family members in fancy or decorated tombs (graves). It is one way they care for their ancestors.

Most other Malagasy are Christians. They go to Catholic and Protestant churches. A small group of Malagasy follows the religion of Islam.

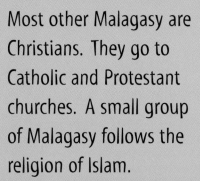

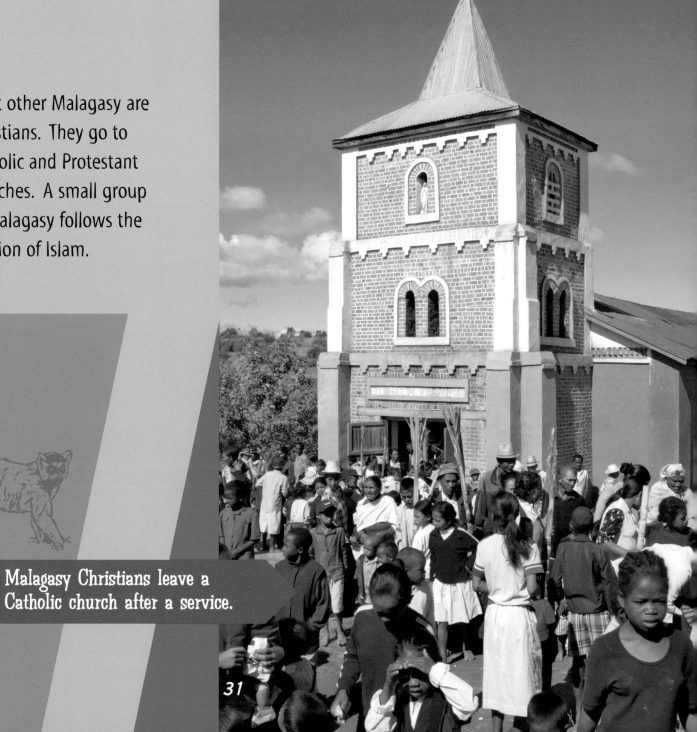

Malagasy Christians leave a Catholic church after a service.

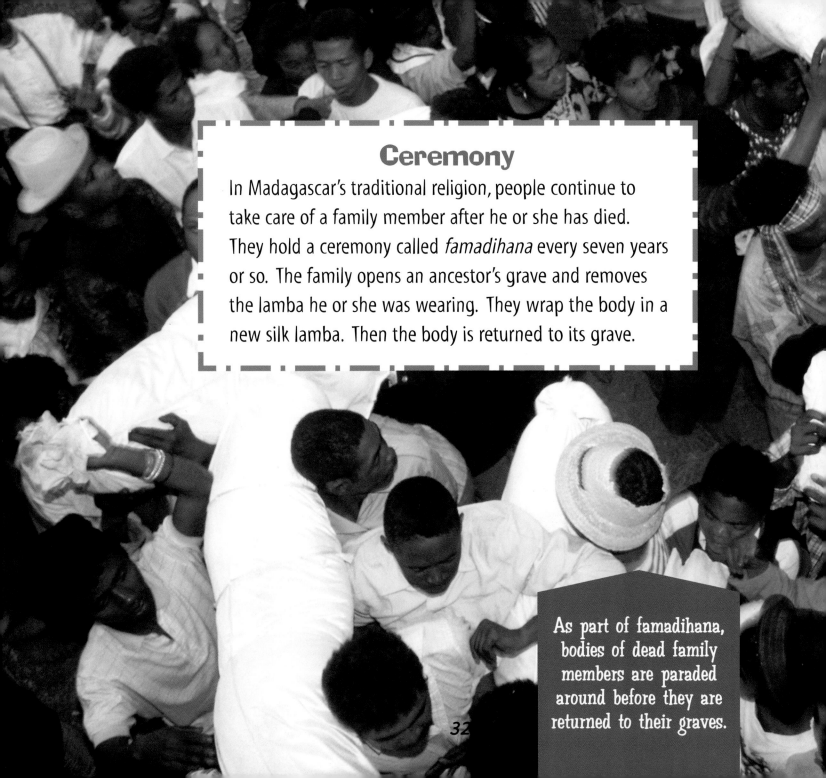

Ceremony

In Madagascar's traditional religion, people continue to take care of a family member after he or she has died. They hold a ceremony called *famadihana* every seven years or so. The family opens an ancestor's grave and removes the lamba he or she was wearing. They wrap the body in a new silk lamba. Then the body is returned to its grave.

As part of famadihana, bodies of dead family members are paraded around before they are returned to their graves.

32

Famadihana is a joyous event for the family. It is like a reunion with the family member. Many guests are invited to join the celebration with the family.

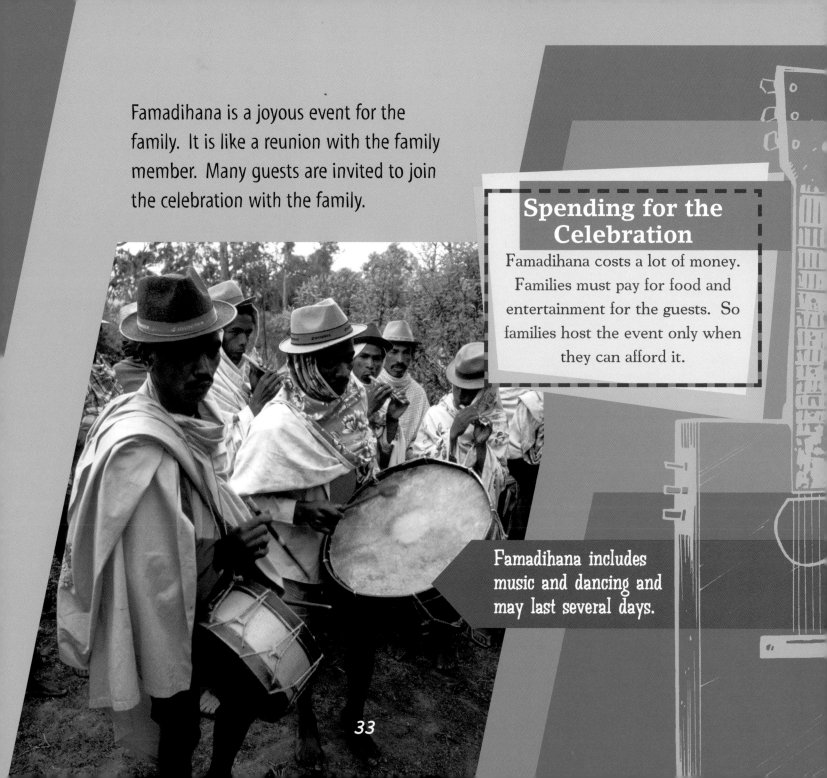

Spending for the Celebration

Famadihana costs a lot of money. Families must pay for food and entertainment for the guests. So families host the event only when they can afford it.

Famadihana includes music and dancing and may last several days.

The Royal Hill of Ambohimanga

Holidays

The traditional Malagasy New Year is called Alahamady. This fun holiday falls in March. On the first day of celebration, people in Antananarivo dress up in lambas. They walk to the highest point in the town. There they give one another gifts, listen to music, and sing. They may even try to talk to their ancestors. The next morning, many Christian Malagasy go to church.

Dear Mom and Dad,

Madagascar is a blast! Yesterday we celebrated Alahamady. We climbed the Royal Hill of Ambohimanga in Tana. Then we listened to loud music and danced in the old queen's palace. Grandma even gave me a lamba to wear over my clothes. It was so fun!

See you soon!

Sarah

34

The Malagasy celebrate their freedom on June 26. France used to rule Madagascar. Madagascar became an independent country in 1960. On Independence Day, schoolchildren sing the national song and parade through the streets. Friends and family get together in the evening to dance and eat.

School

Alarm clocks ring early on school days. Malagasy kids have to make it to class by seven in the morning. All classes are taught in French. Children study English, science, math, history, and geography.

ECOLE PRIMAIRE PUBLIQUE
ZANAKAMBONY MANANDONA ANTSIRABE II

Children stand in front of their elementary school in the highlands.

Fady

In Madagascar, *fady* are things people should not do. These things are disrespectful. Children learn about fady from their families and everyone around them. Here are a few examples of fady:

- Being rude to a stranger
- Refusing a stranger's kindness and hospitality
- Children eating their meals before their elders

These Malagasy children do schoolwork at tables in their classroom.

Rice Is Nice

Rice is the most popular food in Madagascar. Many people eat watery rice for breakfast. Dried meat or fish may be served with it. For lunch and dinner, folks feast on rice with vegetables or stews of chicken, fish, or pork. Chili peppers, salt, curry powder, cloves, and garlic spice up the stews.

This Malagasy dish has zebu meat on skewers and mango slices over rice.

Cooks make a side dish called *lasary voatabia.* It has tomatoes and onions tossed with a lemon and hot pepper sauce. Malagasy enjoy sweet fruits such as bananas and mangoes for dessert.

Madagascar grows a lot of lychee fruit. The fruit is used in many dessert recipes. It is also shipped to other countries.

Tall Tales

Malagasy kids love to listen to folktales. Many stories try to explain how the world came to be. *Ohabolana* are also popular. Malagasy speakers use these short, smart sayings when chatting with friends. An example of ohabolana is, "Do not kick away the canoe that helped you cross the river." That means, "Do not forget the people who helped you become successful in life."

Malagasy often include music in their storytelling.

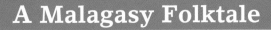

A Malagasy Folktale

Long ago, the Malagasy god Zanahary asked the first man and woman if they would like to die like the moon or like a banana tree. They asked, "What does that mean?"

Zanahary replied, "The moon is always born again. Each month the moon starts out as a sliver and grows bigger. Then it gets smaller until it dies. But the next night it is a sliver again. A banana tree sends off shoots. After the tree dies, the shoots continue to grow into young trees."

The couple decided to die like a banana tree. Because of this, humans have children (like the shoots of a tree). But they have just one lifetime.

Music in the Air

On Sundays, performers in Malagasy villages may hold a *hira gasy*. This is a show that mixes storytelling, singing, and dancing. A speaker welcomes the audience with a speech called a *kabary*. Then actors sing and act out a play. The play teaches the audience a lesson about life. Dancers end the show. They move to the music of blaring horns, pounding drums, and singing violins.

Villagers play instruments to accompany dancers at a festival.

These are traditional Malagasy musical instruments.

THE FLAG OF MADAGASCAR

The flag of Madagascar was adopted in 1958 as the country was gaining independence from France. A white stripe runs down the left side of the flag. A red stripe and a green stripe run left to right at the top and bottom. Red and white were the colors of Madagascar's flag during earlier periods of independence. White stands for purity. Red stands for sovereignty (self-rule). Green was added to represent the common people who fought for independence. The color stands for hope.

FAST FACTS

FULL COUNTRY NAME: Republic of Madagascar

AREA: 226,657 square miles (587,040 square kilometers), or about twice the size of the state of Arizona

MAIN LANDFORMS: the mountain groups Ankaratra and Tsaratanana (parts of the Central Highlands); the cliffs of Angavo and Bongolava; the rain forests along the eastern coast; coastal plains

MAJOR RIVERS: Betsiboka, Mangoky

ANIMALS AND THEIR HABITATS: lemur (forests and throughout); tenrec, fossa, chameleon, ring-tailed mongoose, golden mantella frog (rain forests); tortoise (southern and southwestern dry forests); Nile crocodile (freshwater lakes); coelacanth (ocean water); giraffe weevil (eastern parks)

CAPITAL CITY: Antananarivo

OFFICIAL LANGUAGES: Malagasy, French, English

POPULATION: about 20,654,000

GLOSSARY

ancestors: family members who lived long ago

channel: a narrow strip of sea or ocean between two pieces of land

ethnic group: a group of people with many things in common, such as language, religion, and customs

folktale: a timeless story told by word of mouth from grandparent to parent to child. Many folktales have been written down in books.

mainland: the largest land mass of a country or continent

monsoon: strong, seasonal winds that sometimes carry heavy rainstorms

plain: a large area of flat land

port: a place on the water where ships can dock and load or unload supplies

tradition: a way of doing things—such as preparing a meal, celebrating a holiday, or making a living—that a group of people shares

tropical rain forest: a thick, green forest that gets a lot of rain every year

TO LEARN MORE

BOOKS

Kabana, Joni. *Torina's World: A Child's Life in Madagascar.* Portland, OR: Arnica Publishing, 2008. Large, vivid photos show what daily life in Madagascar is like for children.

Lumry, Amanda. *Mission to Madagascar.* Bellevue, WA: Eaglemont Press, 2005. Explore Madagascar's wildlife as a boy named Riley searches for a rare aye-aye lemur in this illustrated story.

Riley, Joelle. *Ring-Tailed Lemurs.* Minneapolis: Lerner Publications Company, 2009. Read all about Madagascar's most famous animals!

WEBSITES

Madagascar – EnchantedLearning.com
http://www.enchantedlearning.com/africa/madagascar/
This page includes several maps and lots of facts about Madagascar.

A Tour of Madagascar for Kids
http://www.wildmadagascar.org/kids/
This site has bright photos and tons of information on Madagascar's wildlife, history, economy, and more.

Windows on Madagascar
http://www.pbs.org/wgbh/nova/madagascar/explore/windows.html
Click on a photo of a rain forest, village, spiny desert, tomb, or canyonland in Madagascar to find hidden facts about each place.

INDEX